Lucy Moore

Jane Leadbetter

Messy Christmas

Three Complete Sessions and a Treasure Trove of Ideas for Advent, Christmas, and Epiphany

IVP Books

An imprint of InterVarsity Press
Downers Grove, Illinois

InterVarsity Press
P.O. Box 1400, Downers Grove, IL 60515-1426
ivpress.com
email@ivpress.com

InterVarsity Press® is the book-publishing division of InterVarsity Christian Fellowship/USA®, a movement of students and faculty active on campus at hundreds of universities, colleges, and schools of nursing in the United States of America, and a member movement of the International Fellowship of Evangelical Students. For information about local and regional activities, visit intervarsity.org.

All Scripture quotations, unless otherwise indicated, are taken from The Holy Bible, New International Version®, NIV®. Copyright © 1973, 1978, 1984, 2011 by Biblica, Inc.™ Used by permission of Zondervan. All rights reserved worldwide. www.zondervan.com. The "NIV" and "New International Version" are trademarks registered in the United States Patent and Trademark Office by Biblica, Inc.™

Cover design: Cindy Kiple
Images: pine needles: © hydrangea100/iStockphoto
paint spots: © kenkuza/iStockphoto
green ribbon: © JamesBrey/iStockphoto
holiday items: © KarpenkovDenis/iStockphoto
candy cane: © DNY59/iStockphoto

ISBN 978-0-8308-4139-4 (print)
ISBN 978-0-8308-8891-7 (digital)

Printed in the United States of America ∞

InterVarsity Press is committed to ecological stewardship and to the conservation of natural resources in all our operations. This book was printed using sustainably sourced paper.

Library of Congress Cataloging-in-Publication Data
A catalog record for this book is available from the Library of Congress.

| **P** | 37 | 36 | 35 | 34 | 33 | 32 | 31 | 30 | 29 | 28 | 27 | 26 | 25 | 24 | 23 | 22 | 21 | 20 | 19 | 18 | 17 | 16 | 15 | 14 | 13 | 12 | 11 | 10 | 9 | 8 | 7 | 6 | 5 | 4 | 3 | 2 | 1 |
| **Y** | 50 | 49 | 48 | 47 | 46 | 45 | 44 | 43 | 42 | 41 | 40 | 39 | 38 | 37 | 36 | 35 | 34 | 33 | 32 | 31 | 30 | 29 | 28 | 27 | 26 | 25 | 24 | 23 | 22 | 21 | 20 | 19 | 18 | 17 |

For the joyful, ticklish, huggable, and faith-filled Jack, Molly, and Joshua (Lucy).

For L19: Messy Church team, with thanks for all of the Saturdays they give
as God's faithful servants (Jane).

Acknowledgments

Thanks to Denise, Elisabeth Kate, Lesley, and Pete for pulling the ideas apart and rebuilding them.

Contents

Planning Grid for Messy Church 6

Introduction 7

1 Advent Messy Church 9

2 Christmas Messy Church 30

3 Epiphany Messy Church..46

4 Creative Christmas Prayers 61

5 Christmas Extras 70

6 Go for a Green Christmas 73

7 Messy Activity Ideas 76

8 Global Action and Justice at Christmas..78

9 Christmas Games 79

10 Christmas Food Crafts..82

11 Messy Moments Sheets 84

Index of Crafts and Games 94

Planning Grid for Messy Church

Theme: _____   Date: _____

Crafts	Preparation	Craft Leader	Notes

Introduction

Christmas! What a time of contrasts! It's a time of huge strain and stress for many families as we try to afford unaffordable gifts, food, and drink, as well as cope with a break in routine, the grim expectation that we "have to be happy," and the presence of incompatible family members under one roof with no escape route except arguments, over-consumption, and end-to-end immersion in TV . . .

But it's also a time of great celebration, when God gives us the gift of his own self. The story can never be retold often enough of a single mother and a husband suspicious of his wife's unfaithfulness; of the birth of a baby and the hope for outsiders everywhere when outcasts and foreigners come to visit him; of wicked kings and joyful angels; of flights in the dark and light in the darkness. It's a time for excited children and magical moments, for generosity, hospitality, and parties (and particularly good TV). Christmas is a meeting between heaven and earth.

Through these three Messy Church sessions, a local church can help twenty-first-century families own the eternal messages of Christmas for themselves, so that seasonal tensions, sentimentality, and material pleasures have a chance to fall into a better perspective. The three sessions are planned to run once a month for three consecutive months between November and January to encourage families to keep coming back for the next thrilling installment, offering churches the chance to reinforce the learning and provide echoes that will deepen the worship experience over the period. Two of the craft activities deliberately repeat themselves with variations over the three months so that there is a sense of building on the past. You might also like to consider the three sessions as an opportunity to do crafts that take longer, especially for adults and teenagers who might complete a craft activity over three sessions—a chance to "leave things to dry," for example.

We've included a section on extra Christmas craft ideas: Christmas Extras. These crafts don't have detailed explanations but are there to suggest ideas for Christian themes at Christmas time, and you'll easily find instructions on the web. You could use them as alternative crafts at your Messy Church or as a way of extending the usefulness of this book over more than one Christmas season.

The creative prayer ideas encourage families to enjoy praying together and to learn about happiness as they do so.

Our responsibility to look after the world we live in is given practical outworking in the recycling sections and in the global action and justice ideas.

Everyone learns in different ways, so there are sections of ideas for really messy learners and activity-based learning. This means that there is something for all to enjoy and a challenge for everyone.

Finally, the Messy Moments and take-home ideas encourage families to continue their spiritual care for each other at home as well as at gathered church.

Making things together—even simply making a mess together—can be one way in which God's kingdom explodes into life in a church, a community, an individual, or a family. We're not just gluing and sticking: we're reflecting the God who creates and re-creates and gives us the chance to be more fully human as we mirror his actions. Just as God wasn't afraid to get his hands into the stuff of the earth—touch swaddling clothes, skin, and straw; smell frankincense and myrrh; taste milk and bread—the act of making things also gives people a chance to get their hands into the stuff of the earth, to give their senses a feast, to savor what is good, and to feel real things in a screen-based world. Craft time makes a space for adults and children to have time together, to enjoy being a family, to marvel at each other's skills, to help each other, and it gives something to do while conversations flourish with family as well as friends. Alongside the sheer joy of learning new skills, difficult biblical themes and stories can be explored in a non-confrontational way through drawing, splatting, building, and experimenting.

We hope your Messy Church will be a huge and happy gift to your community this Christmas.

Advent Messy Church

- **Theme:** Preparing for Christmas

- **Biblical story:** Mary and Joseph are under immense stress as they prepare for the journey to Bethlehem.

- **Equipping today's families:** Accepting that Christmas is a stressful time for families, but Jesus is at the heart of the celebrations and preparations, and he is ultimately all that matters. Strategies for coping with and pre-empting the stress: Advent is a time of preparation, and preparation for both the material and spiritual sides of Christmas can help to make the season meaningful and enjoyable.

Crafts

Christmas to do list

You will need:

Notebook, attractive paper or cardstock for cover, stickers, sequins, paper shapes for decoration, and a printout of the following words on a piece of paper the same size as the notebook cover:

Jesus said, "Do not worry, saying, 'What shall we eat?' or 'What shall we drink?' or 'What shall we wear?' . . . But seek first his kingdom and his righteousness, and all these things will be given to you as well." (Matthew 6:31, 33)

How to

Decorate a notebook to make lists to help you prepare for Christmas and stay in control of all the busyness. You could write dates of school and social events, to do lists, lists of gifts to buy, addresses, recipes, and so on.

Talk about how busy we all are in the days leading up to Christmas, but how it can help us to stay unstressed if we remember that the only things that really matter are loving God and loving the people around us. Everything else is just icing on the cake. You might offer to pray for anyone who has real worries about making ends meet this Christmas.

Bath bombs

You will need:

A bath bomb-making kit or ingredients (including citric acid, baking soda, cornstarch, witch hazel, food coloring, and fragrances) as listed in one of the many Internet recipes. The kits cost around $20 to make about six bombs.

How to

Mix everything up well and spritz the dry ingredients with witch hazel as per the instructions from the web. You can use molds or just make rough ball shapes in your hands. The bombs take a few hours to dry, so you could invite people back to pick them up next month. Alternatively, buy a kit at your local craft store and follow those instructions.

Talk about taking the time to relax in a nice bath during the busyness of the run-up to Christmas. You could mention that Advent is a time of preparation, and lots of Christians take time out to think about God, life, the universe, and everything during Advent.

Large wreath no. 1

This is the first of three wreaths to be made during the three Messy Church sessions and included in the celebrations.

You will need:

The basis for a wreath that's about six feet in diameter—big enough for people to walk through. Suggestions are a length of tubing twisted into a circle, corrugated cardboard pieces taped together, three dowel rods (this will make a doorway rather than a wreath, but that's okay), or, for those who have woodworkers on the team, a beautiful hollow plywood circle. (Remember, you'll need two more for the next two sessions.)

You will also need old Christmas decorations such as tinsel, paper chains, angels, reindeer, Santas, gift boxes, and so on; plus index cards and pens.

How to

The wreath or doorway can be strung up from beams, strapped upright to a couple of chairs, or held up by volunteers. Be aware of the need for wheelchair, stroller, and walker access.

Decorate this first wreath with secular Christmas decorations on one side. The idea is that these things are fine in themselves and that God wants us to enjoy them but step through them into what Christmas is really all about. You could cover the wreath in double-sided tape so that it's very easy even for toddlers to stick shapes on to it; you can tie on the heavier items.

On the other side will go our worries, preoccupations, jobs to do before Christmas, concerts, parties, and plays that will take up our time. These can be written on the index cards and taped on to the wreath.

Talk about

the things that you're looking forward to about Christmas, and the things that are stressing you out already. Say that God's interested in making these things easier for you, and that's what today's Messy Church is all about.

Pillowcases/stockings

You will need:

Cheap pillowcases and fabric pens, or stocking shapes cut from felt with holes punched along the sides and yarn to thread through in contrasting colors.

How to

As part of getting ready for Christmas, decorate a pillowcase or stocking for yourself or someone in your family to leave out on Christmas Eve. If you are using felt shapes, sew up the stocking by threading the yarn through the holes.

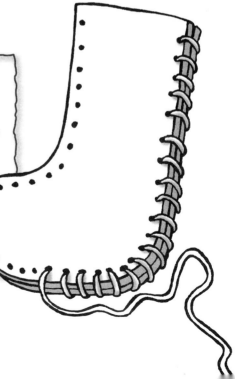

Talk about the anticipation of the run-up to Christmas and how Mary might have felt, waiting for her baby to be born.

Chocolate-covered treats

You will need:

Fair-trade chocolate, non-choking foods in small chunks (for example, pineapple chunks, apple slices, strawberries, balls of fondant icing, halved grapes, banana slices, candy), toothpicks, wax paper, and an icepack placed under the wax paper to help the items set quickly.

How to

Melt the chocolate in a microwave or over hot water (away from children) and dip a piece of food into the chocolate using toothpicks. Place it on the wax paper to set and cool, then eat.

Talk about how, just like these treats, the outside parts of Christmas are great fun—gifts and stockings and parties and plays. But what's hidden on the inside is even better. What do you think is at the heart of Christmas?

Stir-fry vegetable chopping

You will need:

A trained chef, lots of raw vegetables, chopping boards, different sorts of knives, and adult supervision.

How to

Learn to chop properly from your chef and use the chopped vegetables to make a big stir-fry for the meal afterwards.

Talk about the way, in stir-fry meals, it takes time to prepare the food so that the meal tastes great. Christmas is a bit like that: it takes a lot of getting ready, but the getting ready is hugely important to make sure the celebration itself is as meaningful as it can be.

Game: How many people fit on a donkey?

You will need:

Suitcases, a flat cut-out of a donkey, roughly life-size, made out of a material that won't rip easily; or (with plenty of supervision) a 3D "donkey" made of two or three giant exercise balls strapped together.

How to

Put the donkey shape flat on the floor and challenge families to fit as many people and suitcases as they can on to the shape. No part of anyone's body may touch the floor; they have to be completely on the donkey. Watch out for the safety of smaller people!

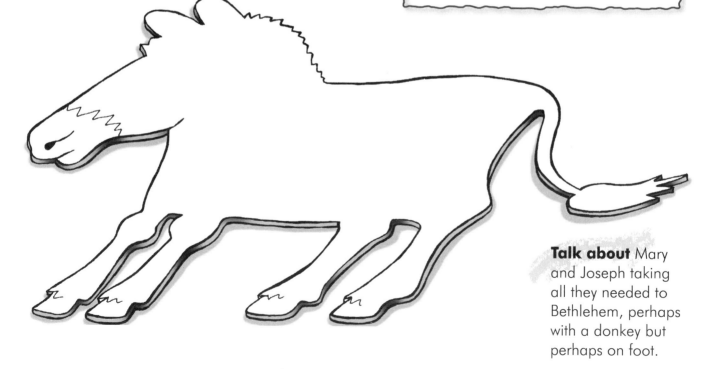

Talk about Mary and Joseph taking all they needed to Bethlehem, perhaps with a donkey but perhaps on foot.

Wall display/bulletin board

This display continues over two sessions.

You will need:

A gold or silver gel pen, a pattern for simple origami boxes (see diagram), paper of different colors in sizes to make a box and a lid (squares of wrapping paper work well), ribbon, glue, and double-sided tape.

How to

Invite people to write a prayer to God on one of the smaller pieces of paper: something they're worried about, something they're thankful for, someone they want God to look after, and something private to them. Make this paper into the base of the box using the origami folding and glue, and make a second, larger piece of paper into the lid, using the same pattern. Fit them together so that the prayer is hidden both in the folds of the paper and under the lid. Write your name over the lid of the box in silver or gold gel pen. Tie it up in ribbon and add it to the wall display using double-sided tape.

Make a new box at this session and the next, and attach them to the wall display.

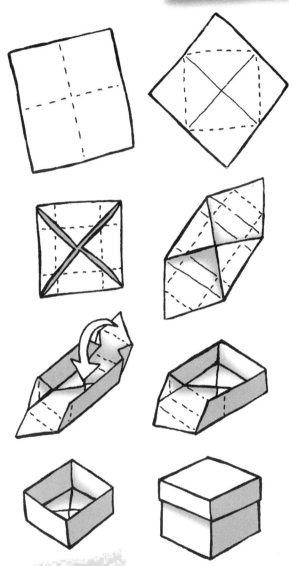

Talk about how much can change over two months. At the end of two months, people can take home their boxes and see what they've been talking to God about over that time.

Upcycle wooden items

This activity could continue over three sessions.

 You will need:

A selection of old wooden chairs, trays, boxes, and so on; fine-grade sandpaper; dish soap and brush or cloth; either acrylic paints or pictures to cut out of comics and magazines for decoupage; wood glue; and varnish.

How to

Sand down the wooden object and clean it with diluted dish soap. Allow to dry. Paint, if this is the only finish you want.

Cut out a selection of pictures if using decoupage. Arrange the cut-outs over the object, then glue them down and smooth off thoroughly to avoid air bubbles.

When dry, varnish with matte varnish using a medium-sized brush following appropriate safety precautions and adult supervision.

Professional varnishing on an item like a chair needs fifteen to twenty coats; you may suggest fewer.

Talk about the care Joseph would have taken in making things out of wood, and how Jesus would have learned from Joseph as he grew up.

Rough log slab stools

You will need:

Sawn-off slices of a tree trunk about three inches thick, small wooden blocks or chunks, strong wood glue, and sandpaper.

How to

Clean up the slab of wood with a damp cloth and some diluted dish soap. Sand down its flat upper surface if it is really rough or splintery. (Leave the bark on.)

Sand down three small chunks of wood, roughly equal in size. On the underside of the slab, glue on the three chunks of wood to be the legs of the stool and leave to dry.

Talk about how rough Joseph's hands would have been from all that woodwork.

Quiet space

Listen to classical music

Research from the Science University of Tokyo shows that classical music is helpful for reducing levels of anxiety and stress. It has been shown to slow down the heartbeat, which helps people to relax, and it stimulates the part of the brain connected with emotional activity and sleep.

Create a comfortable corner or other space with chairs, cushions, and beanbags. Play some quiet classical music (using a CD player or iPod and headphones).

Provide instructions for easy breathing exercises:

- Sit in a relaxed position.
- Slowly inhale through your nose, counting to five in your head.
- Let the air out of your mouth, counting to eight in your head as it leaves your lungs.
- Repeat several times.

Provide some simple coloring pages or a sandpit to occupy small children, at least for a little while, so that stressed parents can relax.

Celebration

As people come in, play or sing your own version of "Deck the Halls." Place the wreath at the doorway so that everyone walks through the wreath to come in. As you talk about the crafts and activities you've just been doing, keep reminding everyone that it's been all about preparations—getting ready: "It's a very busy time of year. Look at all the busy things we've stuck on our wreath! But we get busy now so that we can really enjoy the fantastic gift that God gives us all at Christmas time."

Storyteller:	There was one family who had a huge amount to do.
Joseph:	Hello. I'm Joseph and I've got lots to do: I've got to build a house for me and my fiancée to live in when we get married. She's beautiful! She's kind! I love her so much! *(Ad lib here: invite people to come and help build the imaginary house. Then see Mary coming and send them back to their seats so that you can be alone with Mary.)*
Mary:	Joseph, God told me I'm going to have a baby.
Joseph:	But . . . it's not my baby.
Mary:	No, it's God's baby; a gift to the world.
Joseph:	I need to sleep on this. *(Lies down.)*
Storyteller:	In those days, this was a really big deal. Mary could be stoned to death for having someone else's baby. So Joseph decided to split up from Mary, but to do it quietly so that she wouldn't be killed and people wouldn't talk too much about her. But God needed Joseph as part of his plans. He sent an angel to Joseph. We need the sound of an angel arriving in the night! Can you make it for me? *(All make a whooshing sound.)*
Angel:	Joseph! God needs you to look after Mary and her baby. So get married to her, just as you were planning to. The baby really is God's baby!
Storyteller:	The angel went away, with the same sound. *(All make whooshing sound.)* Joseph woke up.
Joseph:	I suppose I'd better build a bigger house for all three of us.

Storyteller:	It was very tough for them both, as people did talk about Mary. And it got even tougher. The Romans made a proclamation. We need some Roman soldiers to march in!
Roman:	*(Mustering some volunteer soldiers and lining them up to march in.)* Left, right, left, right, left, right . . . HALT! Listen, you horrible bunch of Nazareth people! We're here to tell you you've got to go and fill in your census forms in the town where you were born. Or you'll be in big trouble, won't they, boys?
Soldiers:	Yeah!
Roman:	Attention! Left, right, left, right, left, right! *(Marches them off.)*
Joseph:	Mary, we'll need to get ready to go to Bethlehem. That's eighty miles away!
Mary:	Oh, there's so much to do to get ready for this journey.

We call the start of December Advent. It's a special time of year for getting ready for Christmas. There are things to make and preparations needed for visits with family and friends. It's a very busy time for all of us, just as Mary and Joseph had to get ready for Jesus' birth. So how about showing God how special you think he is by making space for him in all the busyness this year?

Response

Give everyone a nicely designed card, ideally with a magnet on the back so it can be stuck to the fridge at home, with these words on it:

This year we'll prepare for Christmas by making space to . . .

This year we'll prepare for Christmas by making space to...

On the display at the front of the worship space, show some suggestions for ideas to help people live happily as a family, to help them remember Jesus, and to help them to love their neighbors. Choose suggestions from the list below that you think are most appropriate for the families who come to your Messy Church.

- Help each other to say "sorry" when we get stressed.
- Say "I love you" to people in our family once a day.
- Get rid of one bad habit that annoys other people in our family.
- Light a candle once a day to remember what's really important.
- Get an Advent calendar with Jesus on it.
- When we're shopping for food, say "thank you" to Jesus for all that he gives us.
- Buy an Advent book with one thought for each day.
- Read the Christmas story together.
- Through a charity, give a present to children who really need it.
- Give something to our local foodbank.
- Sell some toys and belongings at a rummage sale and give 10 percent of the money to church or another charity.

Invite families to talk about which one thing they want to do as a family to make space for Jesus this year and to write it on their own card. Then invite families to hold the cards together while you pray for them:

> Dear God, November and December can be very stressful and exciting months, with so much to do: the school concerts, the plays, the shopping, and the preparations. Please join us in all the busyness. Help us to get everything done and to remember you are the most important part of Christmas. Amen.

When we ask God for something, he always answers us, so let's watch out for how he helps us this year.

Sing the hymn "O Come, All Ye Faithful" with oodles of percussion and oomph. There are numerous YouTube versions of it, so you could sing along to one of those if you have the technology.

Finish with the Messy Grace:

May the grace of our Lord Jesus Christ (*Hold out your hands as if expecting a gift*)
And the love of God (*Put your hands on your heart*)
And the fellowship of the Holy Spirit (*Hold hands*)
Be with us all now and for ever. Amen! (*Raise hands together on the word "Amen"*)

As families go out through the wreath together, give them a booklet about Christmas or Advent to take home and read.

Cards to put on the meal table

- Which craft did you enjoy most today?
- Who gets more of your sympathy, Mary or Joseph?
- What stresses you out most about the run-up to Christmas?
- What gives you the most hope for the world?
- Which event in your life were you best prepared for?

Take-home ideas

Festive fragrances

To make a stress-relief gift, glue a printed sheet onto the paper bag. Decorate the bag and place inside a clementine, a tealight, and a small piece of pine. Create a calm and comfortable environment with these fragrances in your home, or give the bag as an Advent gift to someone.

You will need:

Paper bags, printed sheets of paper saying "Keep Calm and Carry On," decorating materials (crayons, pens, stickers, and so on), clementines (*not* oranges), pine wood (real Christmas tree branches), and spicy scented tealights.

Other ideas

- **Stress balls:** Buy stress balls or make them by wrapping dried rice in plastic wrap to make a ball shape. Stretch a balloon over the plastic wrap and cut off the neck. Stretch another balloon over, covering the neck hole. Alternatively, stretch a balloon over a ball of playdough and draw an emotional face on it with a permanent marker.

- **Cup of tea:** Enjoy the delights of chamomile tea with family and friends for a soothing few minutes, or discover the fragrances and flavors of other tea types. You could make it doubly special by making tea properly—taking time to choose the right blend of tea leaves, warming the pot, and allowing it to brew for exactly the right length of time. Serve in your best cups or mugs with a single cookie—it's a real slowing-down exercise.

- **Chill-out jigsaw puzzle:** Clear the busy table to make a large jigsaw puzzle space, and invite everyone to place pieces.

- **Chocolate:** Think of others who may be more stressed than you. Buy them a bar of chocolate.

- **Family happy hour:** Ask the family to decide when you could have a happy hour together. What would you choose to do to relax—watch a movie, have a good laugh, cook a meal, share a meal, walk the dog?

- **Messy Nativity:** Take part in a journey that leads you to Christmas: choose a nativity set to pass around the households of your Messy Church during Advent, allowing Jesus and his family to journey through your community and homes. Arrange an event or service for the final day of the journey (such as a Christmas pagent).

- **Read Philippians 4:6-7:** Don't fret or worry but share your concerns with God, who will come to settle you down.

- **Give up on perfection:** Be content and smile about the things you can achieve, even if they are unfinished or rushed.

Messy messages for Advent

Give these messages to your family, post them on your Facebook page during Advent, tweet to your group members each day, or print off and use in Advent calendars.

1. Happy Advent! When you go to school or the store or work today, stop for a second and say "thank you" to God for something good.

2. Tell someone you love them.

3. Nine months of waiting . . . how did Mary cope?

4. Joseph stuck by Mary with God's help. Ask for God's help with someone you're finding difficult.

5. How long ago do you think God decided to come to earth as a baby?

6. The angel said to Mary, "You are truly blessed!" Blessings come in funny packaging. What is your messiest blessing?

7. Mary's cousin Elizabeth no doubt prayed with her and cheered her up. Talk to a friend today. See if they want a prayer said for them.

8. Give someone a hug today.

9. Zechariah said of Jesus, "This light will shine to guide us into a life of peace" (Luke 1:79, paraphrase). Pray for peace in a country you're concerned about.

10. Sort out a messy spot in your home that's bothering you.

11. Eat something delicious today, and take the time to enjoy it properly.

12. Give some money to someone who needs it more than you.

13. Mary and Joseph had to go to fill in the census, but your name is already written in God's book of life.

14. Tell everyone in your family one thing you like about them.

15. Mary and Joseph were engaged to be married. Pray for an engaged couple you know, that they will stick together even when it's tough.

16. Take a long hot bath and relax.

17. Zechariah said, "God's love and kindness will shine upon us like the sun that rises in the sky" (Luke 1:78, paraphrase). You might not be able to see the sun for rain clouds, but it's still there.

18. Jesus started small. Commit one of your small hopes to God today.

19. Make something—a meal, a picture, a gift—and delight in how good you are at making things.

20. God needed Mary and Joseph to work with him. Look out for one way you can be God's hands in the world today.

21. Watch out for God at home, work, or school today.

22. Touch something wooden. Jesus was placed in a wooden manger, sailed in a wooden ship, ate from a wooden table, and died on a wooden cross.

23. The angel said to Mary, "Nothing will be impossible for God!" (Luke 1:37 ESV). Trust him with something that is impossible for you.

24. "How silently, how silently the wondrous gift is given." Look around and see what God's given you.

25. Merry Christmas! May you catch up on sleep after an early start, and may you find a moment to enjoy God with you.

Christmas Messy Church

- **Theme:** Celebrating God's gift in Jesus, which is reflected in our homes and families, and remembering those who have no homes or families.

- **Biblical story:** Jesus' birth when there was "no room at the inn." He was homeless and was visited by the "homeless" shepherds.

- **Equipping today's families:** Expressing gratitude for our own home, family, and Messy Church family, and remembering those with no home or family.

Crafts

Straw bed

You will need:
Strips of yellow and gold paper, pens, and a manger.

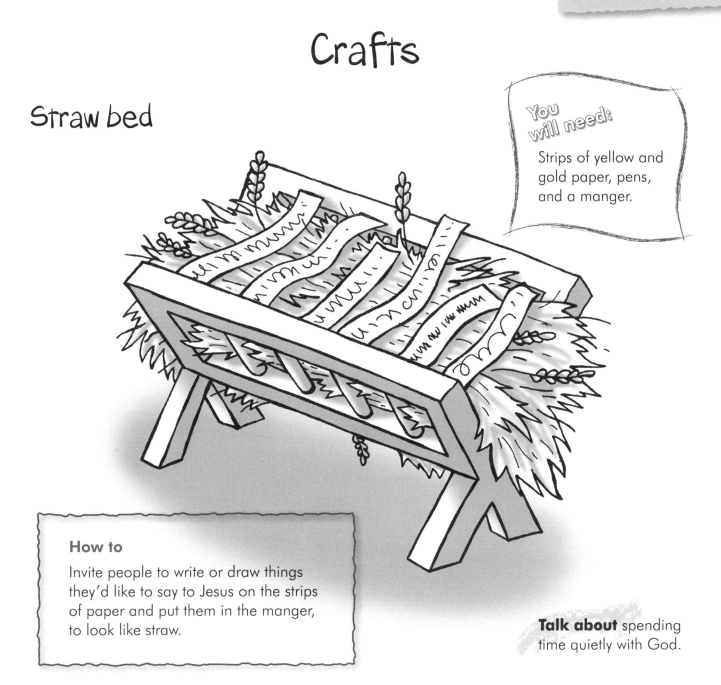

How to

Invite people to write or draw things they'd like to say to Jesus on the strips of paper and put them in the manger, to look like straw.

Talk about spending time quietly with God.

Shelter for the homeless

You will need:

Pictures of cardboard box houses or shelters from newspapers and magazines, large cardboard boxes, long cardboard tubes, and Christmas decorations.

How to

Make a life-sized shelter like the ones in the magazine pictures. Add some decorations.

Talk about: How do you think it feels to be living somewhere like this at Christmas time? How does it make you feel when you add the decorations?

Large wreath no. 2

You will need:

A wreath base (see page 12), lots of glitter, tinsel, garland, shiny foil, shiny ribbon, white cardstock angels, and so on for one side; pictures of refugees, asylum seekers, and homeless people on the streets for the other.

How to

Cover the wreath with one side representing the glory of heaven and the brilliance of the angels, and the other side representing the homelessness that Jesus knew from a very early age.

Talk about: Why do you think Jesus would leave his home in the glory of heaven and come to earth to be a homeless person?

Fingerprint family

You will need:

Inkpads, cardstock or paper, glue and glitter, and pens.

How to

Make a fingerprint for each member of your family (however you understand family—it could be nuclear family, extended family, or church family). The fingerprint makes the body and, using a pen, you can add the arms, legs, and face of each person. Dribble glue around the edge of the cardstock or paper and dust with glitter for a frame.

Talk about: Who is in Jesus' family?

Shepherds picture

Dark-colored paper, glue, glitter, paper people cut-outs to color or paint as shepherds and angels, orange paint, and cotton balls.

How to

Make a starry sky using glitter sprinkled over glue blobs on the dark paper. Stick on people cut-outs, colored or painted as shepherds, and a huge angel. Make sheep out of cotton balls and add a fire with orange paint. If you're feeling ambitious, you could make a rip in the sky and have a host of glittery angels popping out.

Talk about

how the angels made sure these unimportant people knew that Jesus had been born, before anyone else did.

Angel costumes

You will need:

Anything white, silver or gold—fabric, cardstock, elastic, glitter, or foil; twisting balloons, and homemade templates for wings and a halo.

How to

Invite everyone to make any part of an angel costume—halo, wings, belt, robe, armor, and sword made of twisting balloons. This will be useful for the celebration, and for a Christmas pageant or similar event, if you want to invite families to it in costume. As ever, make sure the adults get included too.

Talk about: What do you think angels look like, compared with the pictures on Christmas cards?

Wall display/bulletin board

You will need:

Gold or silver gel pen, origami box pattern (see p. 17), squares of white or silver paper, ribbon, glue dots or double-sided tape.

How to

Invite people to add another prayer gift box to the display. This time, ask them to see if they can remember how to make the boxes, and to write down something they want to bring to God about their own family this month.

Talk about family life.

Homeless collection box

Shoebox-sized boxes, paper to cover them, sticky-backed paper or wallpaper in the pattern of bricks (optional), stickers of flowerboxes, flowers, and anything else homey.

How to

Decorate the box to look like a house. Make it Christmas-themed if you want to. Cut a slit in the lid and use the box to collect money over the next month for a local or national homelessness charity. Alternatively, take the box home and fill it with goods for your local foodbank, home for young moms, or shelter for the homeless.

Talk about why our Messy Church should help people in need.

White Christmas from Australia

You will need:

Three cups of rice crispies, one cup of mixed dried fruit, one cup of shredded coconut, one cup of powdered milk, three-fourths cup of powdered sugar, coconut cream, and one teaspoon vanilla.

Talk about Christians celebrating Christmas all around the world, in cold seasons and in hot seasons. They are all celebrating the same gift— God's gift of baby Jesus.

How to

To make these treats, put rice crispies, mixed dried fruit, shredded coconut, powdered milk, and powdered sugar together in a bowl. Add vanilla and enough coconut cream to stick it all together, and mix well. Press mixture firmly into a baking tray. Set in a refrigerator, then cut into squares.

In a Messy Church context, you could simply have the ingredients in separate bowls. Each person can put a spoonful of each item in their own bowl and mix it up with a teaspoonful of the coconut cream with vanilla.

Make sure you check your group for coconut allergies.

Ice sculpture

You will need:

A bag of ice cubes on a tray, several boxes of sugar cubes, a little runny icing, and paper plates.

How to

Challenge people to build an igloo out of the ice cubes. It's very hard—in fact, it will probably be impossible—but it's good to do for the feeling of sheer coldness on your hands. When they give up, let people try building one out of sugar cubes and icing "glue" on paper plates instead—infinitely satisfying.

Talk about being homeless and cold, or about countries where the weather at Christmas is different from where you live.

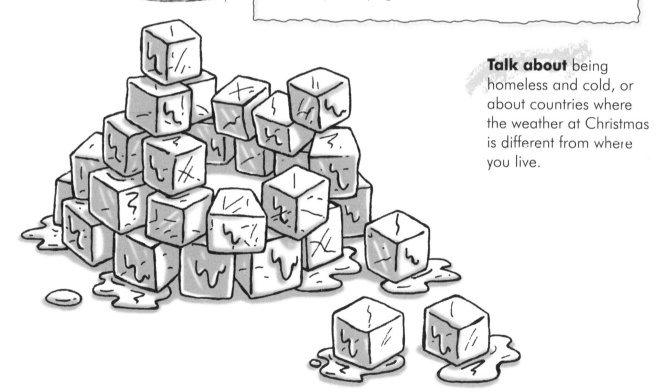

Quiet space

Homelessness

Borrow a very large cardboard box or make a cardboard construction big enough for someone to sit inside. Turn the box on its side with the opening at the front and completely cover it in a dark sheet or blanket. Stick sheets of hologram shiny wrapping paper on the inside walls of the box. Place a flashlight (switched off) and a small blanket inside.

Make an instruction card to read as follows:

Enter the cardboard box and find the flashlight. Sit down and imagine how it must feel to live in a box on the streets. Imagine the weather is cold and damp. How would you keep warm? Place the small blanket around your shoulders. How would you feed yourself? How would you keep clean? Shine the flashlight on the hologram papered walls. Shine the light of Jesus on to the walls and think of all the houses in your neighborhood. Thank God for your homes and pray for those who are homeless. Turn the flashlight off and leave for the next person.

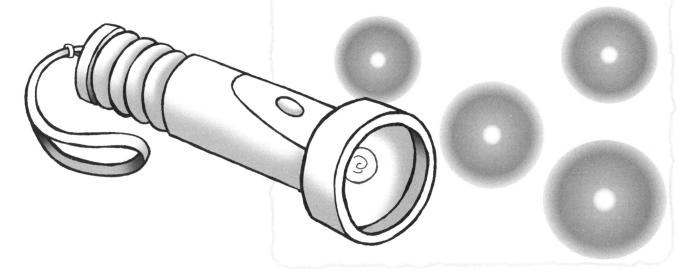

Celebration

Place the Advent busyness wreath in the same place at the doorway of the church or worship space for everyone to walk through again.

Set up the new Christmas wreath of glory near the focal point of your celebration—the front of church or similar—and invite people to walk through this one, too, to enter the worship space.

As you talk about the crafts you've been making, mention how many wreaths we've walked through to get here. Some people stop at the busy wreath and never go any further into the wonder of Christmas, but today we've all come through the wreath of glory as well to see what God wants to show us, hear what he wants to tell us, and take what he wants to give us. We're going deeper into Christmas.

Storyteller: Do you remember? We left Mary and Joseph getting ready for their journey to Bethlehem for the Roman census. Do you remember how far the journey was? Yes, eighty miles! And when they got there, they had a nasty surprise.

Joseph: Have you got a room for the night, please?

Innkeeper 1: We're all full! Sorry!

Joseph: Have you got a room? My wife's expecting a baby . . .

Innkeeper 2: We're so full, we've got three camels sleeping in the bath.

Joseph: Any room?

Innkeeper 3: Only if you can fit in a room with five Roman soldiers, six gladiators, seventeen sumo wrestlers, and a man with really bad breath.

Mary: Joseph! The baby's on its way!

Joseph: Keep breathing, Mary! Any room?

Joseph asks around the congregation until someone says, "Yes!" (In case no one does, have someone primed.)

Joseph: Oh, thank you, God! This person says we can sleep in his stable, Mary!

Storyteller: That night, the baby was born. Mary wrapped him in strips of cloth and laid him in the animals' feed box, as there was nowhere else to put him. But Mary and

Joseph weren't the only ones sleeping rough that night. Out on the hills outside Bethlehem were some very smelly, sweaty, stinky shepherds who hadn't been near a bath for months. They lived outside with the sheep. Would anyone like to come and be a shepherd? *(Invite all shepherds to the front.)* But as they were settling down by the campfire, they got a shock.

Shepherd: What's that?

Angel: Don't be afraid! I've got some wonderful news for you. The baby who will grow up to save the world has been born, and you can go and see him. He's in Bethlehem, in a stable, in a feed box.

Storyteller: Suddenly the sky filled with angels, all shouting praises to God.

Encourage anyone in the congregation who is wearing an angel costume to stand and shout "Praise God" as loud as they can.

Storyteller: Once the angels had gone, the shepherds ran down to Bethlehem to see the baby who would save the world. And when they found him, they knelt down.

Shepherds: Thank you, God!

Storyteller: The baby wasn't in the king's palace or a fancy hotel. He was as homeless and poor as the shepherds were.

Ask a leader to pray:

Thank you, Jesus, for our homes. We're so grateful that we have somewhere to live. Please help those who are anxious about where they are going to live. Amen.

Say, "Some of us have written prayers that are in baby Jesus' manger. Would anyone like to come and read a prayer? We'll all say Amen." Have a few of the prayers read out, with a microphone to help with volume.

If you are collecting for a homeless charity, this would be a good time to describe it briefly and invite people to consider giving some money toward it.

Sing a lively version of one verse of a Christmas carol, such as "Hark! The Herald Angels Sing," or ask everyone which song they would like to sing to God. End with the Messy Grace (see p. 24).

As people leave, invite them to go out through the wreath of glory and look at the other side of it, where there are reminders about homelessness. Christmas is about both sides, and both matter to God. You might give them a leaflet about a local homeless charity or give them a tiny gift as a reminder of the story, such as a knitted sheep or a pencil with a Bible verse on it.

Cards to put on the meal table

- What was your favorite part of the celebration?
- If you were homeless, what would the worst part be for you: (a) loneliness, (b) the cold, or (c) the danger?
- What does your community do for the homeless?
- What would you most like your family to remember about this Christmas?
- What's the best part about Christmas for you?

Take-home ideas

- **Donate:** Clean out and donate your old clothes and other possessions to your local homeless shelter.

- **Hamper:** Make a laundry hamper to donate to a refugee or homeless shelter. Include a card to say that you are praying for them.

- **Plaque:** Thank God for your home. Make a "God bless this home" plaque together.

- **Talk about** which room in your house is your favorite and why.

- **Read Matthew 25:31-45** about showing hospitality to the needy.

- **Christmas crackers:** Personalize homemade Christmas crackers (decorated cardboard tubes) by including a photo, with a magnetic strip attached for the fridge door, and a silly joke. Grandparents will love it.

- **Portrait:** Arrange for a family portrait photo to be taken.

- **Hospitality:** Make extra room for someone else on Christmas Day. Who may be alone at this time?

- **Album:** Create a family photo album to celebrate the Christmas season. Add thoughts, recipes, trips out, and so on. Decorate the pages with festive cut-outs and stickers.

- **White Christmas:** Collect white chocolates and candy to wrap in clear cellophane, tied with a ribbon and a "White Christmas" label/tag. Place one on the Christmas meal table for each person on Christmas Day.

- **Carol singing:** If you love singing, find out about any organized Christmas carol singing groups (perhaps the Scouts, church, or Rotary Club) and make inquiries about joining.

- **Wreath:** Make an edible Christmas wreath together. Make a base of styrofoam or cardboard painted in a festive color. Glue wrapped candy all over the base, overlapping them to make it look really full.

- **Table wreath:** Spike soft candy with toothpicks and use them to decorate a table centerpiece that can be eaten fairly quickly.

Epiphany Messy Church

- **Theme:** Being a light in our own homes.

- **Biblical stories:** The wise men meeting Jesus and returning home with the light; the slaughter of the innocent children.

- **Equipping today's families:** Encouragement and practical ways to be lights in home and family: reconciliation, forgiveness, fun, gratitude, blessing, delight, and love. Also, remembering those who have dangerous childhoods.

Crafts

Thank you notes

 You will need:

Nice plain notepaper in A5 size (about 5.8 inches by 8.3 inches), hole punchers in different designs, a stamp saying "Thank you," and an inkpad.

How to

Fold the notepaper in half to make a greeting card shape. Use the hole punchers to decorate the edge of the paper and, if desired, glue on the paper shapes punched out of your own or other people's notepaper. Stamp at least one "Thank you" on the paper. Use the notepaper to write a thank you letter for Christmas gifts.

Talk about being grateful for all the good things we are given.

Tea light holders

You will need:

Glass jars, glue, sand, masking tape, and tea lights.

How to

Stick squares of masking tape all around the jar, leaving gaps between the squares. Paint the jar generously in glue and roll it in sand. Allow it to dry, then peel off the masking tape to leave windows. Place a tea light inside and, when lit, it should shine through the windows.

Talk about how Jesus' light can shine out of your home through the way you live as a family.

Salty house

You will need:

Coarse salt, glue, cardstock, ribbon or string, and hole punch.

How to

Cut out a simple house or block of apartments shape from the cardstock, about four inches high. Punch a hole in the top. Coat both sides with glue and sprinkle on the salt to cover it on both sides. Allow to dry, and thread a ribbon through the hole to use as a hanger.

Talk about salt sparkling and reflecting the light, just as our homes can reflect the light of Jesus out into our street.

Hand massage

You will need:

Massage oil containing frankincense or myrrh.

How to

Give someone a hand massage using the same precious spices that the wise men brought to Jesus as a gift. (Watch out for sensitive skin and allergies.)

Talk about the smell.

Wise man's star bookmark

You will need:

Gold embroidery yarn, short lengths of dark blue or black felt, and needles.

How to

Learn an embroidery stitch that might have been used to decorate a wise man's cloak with stars, and use it to decorate a bookmark with as many stars as you want. (Younger children could sew yarn across holes punched in cardstock.)

- Stitch the bottom-left to top-right diagonal of an X.
- Stitch the bottom-right to top-left second diagonal of the X.
- Stitch a top-to-bottom bar across the center.
- Stitch a horizontal left-to-right bar across the center.

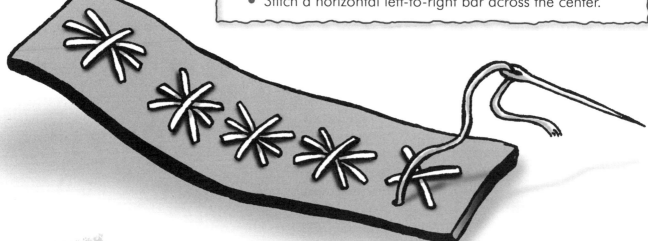

Talk about the wise men following the star in search of Jesus. How far would you go for him?

Mirror mobile

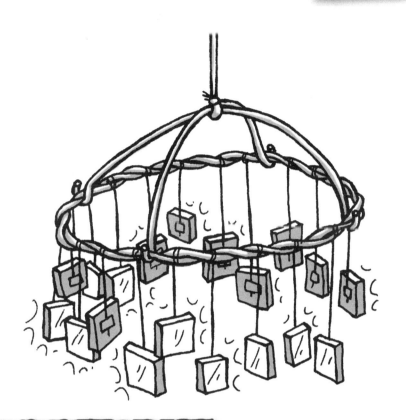

How to

Make a supporting circle of wire, twisted to be strong enough to hold its shape. Make a handle or hanger above this circle, also out of wire.

Cut two to four inch lengths of wire and tape one end of each on to the back of a mirror tile. Attach the other end to the wire circle.

Hold the completed vibrating circle of mirrors over and around a lit bulb, and see them reflect the light.

Talk about dark places you know of, and how God's light shines into them.

Large wreath no. 3

This is the third and final wreath—a sending out wreath with foil cardstock arrows on it. It sends us back to our homes, schools, and workplaces to take the light of Jesus with us into the new year.

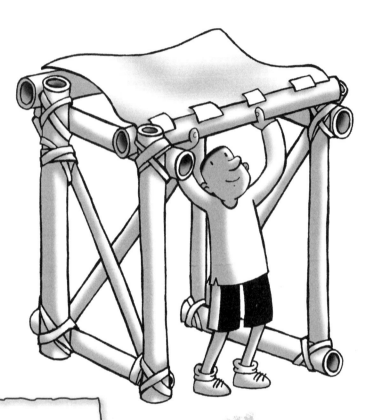

You will need:

Long cardboard tubes (for example, from a carpet showroom); duct tape; pictures of lights, candles, bulbs, flashlights, lighthouses, headlights, laser beams, and any other light sources from magazines and catalogs; and shiny cardstock (or plain cardstock and aluminium foil).

How to

Build the outline of a house out of the cardboard tubes—a hollow cube big enough to walk through, held together with duct tape. Decorate it with pictures of light and with shiny arrows pointing out through the house toward the other side (all pointing the same way). If you're feeling very ambitious, you could cover it with fairy lights that actually light up.

Talk about: Explain that this season is called Epiphany, which means the sudden appearance of God, a revelation, or seeing something suddenly that you hadn't seen before. Jesus was revealed to the wise men as God.

Forgiveness plaque

You will need:

Either old forks or plastic disposable forks, pieces of firm backing cardboard, tags or ribbon, awl or other means of punching holes, markers, decorative gems, and sequins (optional).

How to

This craft might be more suitable for older people, otherwise you will need to explain the joke to kids that "fork + giveness = forgiveness." Make a plaque to remind the family to forgive each other, and thus to keep the light of Jesus shining in their home.

Punch holes in the backing cardboard so that you can use ribbon or tags to attach a fork on the left, then a plus sign and the letters "giveness." Decorate the fork with gems or sequins as desired.

Talk about:

Often the best way of living out what we believe as Christians is simply to show forgiveness to people who hurt us. Suggest that people keep the plaque in a room where it will remind everyone to forgive each other.

Wall display/bulletin board

You will need:

Gray paper, black or blue paper, gold ribbon or paper strips.

How to

Ask people to cut the shape of their house out of the black or blue paper and stick it on the gray background. Glue on strips of gold ribbon or paper, pouring out of the windows. Cut out letters to make a title: "Our homes: beacons of blessing."

Our homes : beacons of blessing

Talk about how your home can be a beacon of blessing to your street or community.

Edible stars

Talk about hopes for this year and the star that guided the wise men to Jesus.

You will need:

Plastic molds or ice cube trays in the shape of stars; edible glitter (optional); Fair-trade white chocolate; chocolate or vanilla ice cream; a freezer, freezer blocks (frozen), or a little table-top fridge. (Instead of chocolate, you could use the chocolate sauce that sets instantly when in contact with ice cream, although a fair-trade version might not be available.)

How to

Dust a little edible glitter, if you are using it, into the base of the star-shaped molds.

Melt the chocolate and carefully spoon some into the mold to a depth of one or two inches. Using a teaspoon handle, smear the chocolate up the sides of the mold to make a hollow star-shaped bowl.

Put the chocolate in the freezer for a minute to set, then reinforce with more chocolate if needed, to make stronger walls for the star. Freeze again.

With the chocolate star still in the mold, squish in enough ice cream to fill it up. Freeze briefly, then turn out and eat.

Quiet space

Safety for children

On a large low table, provide a large selection of pictures of toddlers and babies cut from magazines, catalogs, and postcards. Have some dolls of all colors and both genders, and a selection of shoeboxes, toy beds, and small blankets. Use information from Compassion International, World Vision, or a similar charity to highlight the plight of children from different parts of the world who have dangerous upbringings. Some people may wish to pray for children in specific countries. Others may want to pray for children by tucking up a doll safely in a bed as a symbol of safety and security.

Celebration

Set up the wreaths after everyone has arrived. Today, people will go out, not come in, through them.

Talk about today's crafts and activities: they've all been about some visitors who not only met Jesus but also took the light of God's message back to their homes.

Storyteller: Some scientists lived in the East and studied the stars. One night, they saw a star that, they believed, meant that a great king had been born in the kingdom of the Jews. They packed their bags and left to find this great king for themselves.

Wise man 1: We'll go and ask at the palace. That's where kings are born, isn't it?

Encourage "Oh no it isn't" from the congregation.

Wise man 2: Well, we have to look for him somewhere! Let's go and ask King Herod.

Encourage shouts of "No! No!"

Wise man 3: Oh mighty King Herod, can you tell us where the great king has been born? We saw his star in the East and we've come to worship him.

Herod: I'M THE KING! Nobody is king here except me! Let me talk to my advisers. *(To congregation)* Where do the holy books say that the Messiah will be born?

Encourage congregation to answer, "Bethlehem."

Herod: Then why don't you go to Bethlehem to find this . . . king. And when you find him, come and tell me, so that I can come and *(ahem)* worship him too.

Wise man 1: Certainly. Good idea, eh?

Encourage shouts of "No!"

Storyteller: The wise men traveled to Bethlehem, and their star shone out over the place where Joseph, Mary, and Jesus were staying. They went in and knelt down in front of Jesus and gave him gifts, which were . . .

Encourage congregation to reply, "Gold, frankincense, and myrrh."

Storyteller: Then they traveled back home to tell everyone there about Jesus. But God warned them not to tell King Herod where Jesus was, and when King Herod realized he had been tricked . . .

Herod: Soldiers! I can't have another king growing up! Go to Bethlehem and kill all the boys who are two years old or younger!

Storyteller: There were many families crying that night because of Herod's cruelty. Mary, Joseph, and Jesus got away with God's help and escaped to Egypt, where they lived until Herod died. Then they came back to Nazareth, where Jesus could grow up safely.

Make the following three prayer stations:

- A dark sheet of cardstock or paper with one big star glued on, and a basket of smaller stars (star stickers or stars punched out of paper).
- A picture of the wise men's gifts in the middle of a large sheet of paper, and a basket of squares of wrapping paper to represent gifts.
- A picture of a crying face with blank space around it, and a basket of pens.

Say, "Because there are so many journeys in today's story, our prayers are going to be a journey too. We invite you to journey around the three prayer stations from today's story and pray as a family or with a friend.

"At the star, stick a star onto the night sky as a sign that you want to go where God leads you this year. At the three gifts, add a gift to the pile and tell Jesus what you want to give him. At the sad face, draw a teardrop on the paper as a prayer to ask God to help all the children who are growing up in danger."

Play some quiet music while people add their prayers at the three stations.

To bring everyone back together, sing or play a song such as "I Have Decided to Follow Jesus," "Shine, Jesus, Shine," or "We Three Kings."

Say the Messy Grace (see p. 24) and explain that you'd like people to go to the meal in family groups through the three wreaths, as there's something for each family to receive after the last wreath.

Place a team member at each wreath to remind families of what they stand for: first the one that reminds us how many preparations we made for Christmas, then the one that shows the glory of the gift of Jesus at Christmas, and finally the one that shows the way out into the new year, holding the light of Jesus as we go into our homes, schools, and places of work. As each family walks through the final wreath together, give them a candle or glow stick (with health and safety precautions in place) and pray a blessing for them as a family, such as the following:

I pray that God will fill your home with the light of his love, and that you will find ways to shine it out everywhere you go this year.

Cards to put on the meal table

- What was the best thing about today's Messy Church?
- If your family was a type of light, would it be (a) a lighthouse, (b) a candle, or (c) a laser? Why?
- What would you travel a long way for?
- What's your main hope for this year?
- What are you most grateful for from this recent Christmas?

Take-home ideas

- **Party:** Hold a family "undecorating" party during the first week of January and, as you take down the Christmas decorations, discuss how you spent Christmas and whether or not you will make any changes next year.

- **Star:** After taking down the decorations, make a large star and hang it up. Read Matthew 2:1-12. Leave the star in your home until the beginning of Lent as a reminder that Jesus is the light of the world.

- **Read Ephesians 5:8-10:** "For you were once darkness, but now you are light in the Lord. Live as children of light (for the fruit of the light consists in all goodness, righteousness and truth) and find out what pleases the Lord."

- **Explore:** Visit www.origami-resource -center.com/stars.html for folded stars you can make together.

- **Stargazing:** Google "stargazing" and explore the night sky. Watch for clear nights and observe the constellations together. If someone in the family has an iPhone, you could download a stargazing or planets app and use it to spot the constellations.

- **Home blessing:** A traditional custom is to create a home blessing on black paper or a small chalkboard to keep by your front door. Bless it by saying, "Let us pray. O Lord God, bless this sign to make it helpful to us. Grant that we who use it with faith and enter our home may enjoy good health and spiritual protection. Through Jesus Christ, our Lord. Amen." Write the year, with the inscription CMB (the initials of Caspar, Melchior, and Balthazar, the traditional names of the three wise men) in between. An example of the popular form of this inscription is: 20+C+M+B+18. It remains above the doorway until Pentecost. Make a frame for the blessing and decorate it.

Creative Christmas Prayers

"Tidings of comfort and *joy*": Christmas is a time to be joyful, to be happy. We can see the Christmas season as a time to learn to be happy, and to equip the families in our churches to be happy. These prayer ideas with a Christmas twist are based on the eight "secrets" from the excellent practical book by Paul Griffiths and Martin Robinson, *The 8 Secrets of Happiness* (Lion Hudson, 2009), adapted where necessary for families and children to do together in church, at a quiet prayer table during the craft time at Messy Church, or at home.

Count your blessings

Group prayer

Counting down to Christmas involves the numbers one through twenty-four. Write these out on a sheet of paper and, together, make a list of twenty-four things you are grateful for. You could stand in a circle and call them out in turn really quickly, with a big "THANK YOU, LORD!" at the end.

Prayer table family prayer

"What does it mean to be blessed? It means to be in a place where you are aware of and appreciate the precious gifts of life that have been given to you" (*The 8 Secrets of Happiness*, p. 27). Show a pile of boxes wrapped as Christmas presents. Provide a set of Christmas tree star ornaments, and, as you hang each one on a Christmas tree, say thank you for the "precious gifts of life" you have been given.

Home prayer

Do a thank you "call" to God. Tell God one thing you're thankful for at the end of each day, or add one item each day to an ongoing "thank you" letter to God.

Practice acts of kindness

Group prayer

Show a cross-section drawing of a home with each room visible, ideally with Christmas decorations drawn in every room. Invite everyone to choose one room and draw or write on a sticky note how they could be kind in that room during Christmas, then stick it onto the picture. Gather the prayers with an invitation to Jesus to help us actually do those kind acts.

Prayer table family prayer

Make copies of outlines of two hands, with one word written on each finger as follows: smile, words, listen, help, time, money, wisdom, surprise, give, and celebrate. Prayerfully think about how you could be deliberately kind, with one or more of these words as your inspiration in the Christmas season. (For example: "give" could mean letting someone else go first in a line.) You could write your chosen word(s) as a reminder on your finger(s).

Home prayer

Start a Christmas tradition in your home to give one gift to someone you don't know. It might be via a charity such as Toys for Tots, sending an animal to a developing country, or it could be giving a gift to someone in your neighborhood.

Savor life's joys

Group prayer

Give everyone an item to eat, and invite them to pause and really savor the different flavors and textures. Now ask everyone to think about a person in their family they're going to see this Christmas. Just as you did with the food item, take a moment to think what you really enjoy about being with that person, and thank God for the time you'll have with them this year.

Prayer table family prayer

On the prayer table, place a set of cards showing words or pictures to represent some or all of the following: family, work, TV, Facebook, video games, community, school, home, clothes, food, pets, sports, dance, exercise, friends, Brownies, Cubs, Scouts, book club, shopping, eBay, books, holidays, music, Christmas Day, and any other aspects of life that are relevant to people around you. Invite everyone to sort the cards into two piles: one for things that only matter in this life, and one for things that matter in this life and on into eternity. Ask for God's help to see the eternal in the everyday.

Home prayer

Eat a special meal together with a properly set table, a candle, and a vase of flowers from the garden—and no TV.

Thank a mentor

Group prayer

Explain that, after Christmas, we say "thank you" for the gifts we've been given, and now we're going to say "thank you" for people we're grateful for. Standing or sitting in a circle, throw or roll a soft stuffed Christmas stocking, squishy festive dog toy, or something similar (anything Christmas-themed and soft) from one person to another across the circle. Each person who catches it says something they appreciate about someone in their life. The leader draws the activity to a close with a short gathering prayer along the lines of "For all these people, Lord, we thank you."

Prayer table family prayer

Set up a "Nazareth to Bethlehem" scene on the table, with a road and a flashlight or candle shining to light the way down the road. Make Joseph and Mary out of playdough and place them on the road. (You could add "dangerous places" to the sides of the road if you like.) Invite families to make themselves out of playdough and place themselves on the road, with the light of God guiding them. Talk about what it looks like to go on the journey with the holy family, and thank God for being "a lamp for my feet, a light on my path" (Psalm 119:105) to Mary and Joseph as well as to you.

Home prayer

Talk about someone God has put in your life, like a surprise Christmas gift, who has really helped or guided you. (Grandma? Great-grandad? A teacher? A social worker? A school crossing guard? A playgroup leader? A friend?) Write that person a postcard or letter to say "thank you" for the special help they've given you. Younger members of the family could decorate the card. Then take it to that person and read it to them.

Learn to forgive

Group prayer

Make a stack of small Christmas-themed gift boxes or gift bags, with a picture inside of the baby in the manger and the words, "The gift of forgiveness: name him Jesus because he will save his people from their sins." Say that God has a great gift to give to every single person who wants it. Invite someone to come and open a gift box and describe what's inside. Warn everyone that, once you've received this gift, you have to use it, because Jesus later prayed, "Forgive us our sins, as we forgive those who sin against us." God gives us the gift of forgiveness but we have to forgive other people too. Tell them, "If you would like the gift, come and take one for free, and, if you think you'll have a problem with using it, ask someone here to talk it through with you."

Prayer table family prayer

The angel told Joseph to call the baby *Jesus* (which means "The Lord saves") "because he will save his people from their sins" (Matthew 1:21). On one side of a slate or chalkboard, draw something you know you need forgiveness for. On the other side, draw something you need to forgive someone else for. Pray, "Forgive us our sins, as we forgive those who sin against us," then wipe the slate clean. (You could do this with pencil and eraser, or with dry erase boards and markers.)

Home prayer

Postal workers bring a lot of cards and boxes during the Christmas season. Invite one member of the family to put a large card or packet through the mailbox flap, but not to let go. Can they pull their hand out again, or are they stuck? The only way they can get free is to let go of what they're holding.

Invest time and energy in friends and family

Group prayer

In family or friendship groups (making sure no one is on their own), tell one another one dream or hope that you have for the Christmas season, and take the time and trouble to really listen to everyone else's. It doesn't matter if they seem like silly or trivial dreams—what matters is listening and being grateful for the privilege of sharing a little of someone else's "secret garden" of dreams.

Prayer table family prayer

Light tea lights in a sand tray for members of your family, asking the light of Jesus to shine in their lives this Christmas.

Home prayer

Make or buy a photo holder with twelve spaces for photos and decorate it to be Christmas-themed. Put photos of family members and friends you won't see over Christmas in the frames and spend a moment on each of the twelve days of Christmas praying for each one in turn.

Take care of your body and soul

Group prayer

Find an upbeat version of a Christmas carol and do an exercise routine together as part of your worship, praising God with every part of your body and soul.

Prayer table family prayer

Find a selection of attractive blank cards with Christmas-themed designs on them and encourage families to think of one thing they could do together this month that would be good for their body or soul. Write it on the card and invite the family to take it home and try to do it during this month.

Home prayer

Together, learn a simple prayer to say at bedtime during Advent or Epiphany, such as the following:

Deep peace of the running wave to you,
Deep peace of the flowing air to you,
Deep peace of the quiet earth to you,
Deep peace of the shining stars to you,
Deep peace of the Son of Peace to you, forever.

Early Scottish, source unknown

Develop strategies for coping with stress and hardship

Group prayer

Ask God to prepare everyone for any problems or sadness at Christmas. Add a link to a festive paper chain for each person you pray for and hang it on the church Christmas tree.

- Christmas is a family time: pray for people who have family issues, have a family member missing, or are on their own.
- Christmas is a time for giving: pray for people who are worried about money matters.
- Christmas is a time for eating great food: pray for those who dread the preparation, cooking, or eating of Christmas dinner, and for those who don't have enough food.
- Christmas is a time for children: pray for anyone who is sad because children are not with them, or because they are lonely.

Prayer table family prayer

Face up to a problem in your life at the moment. Place a traditional nativity scene on the prayer table and talk about how it looks so calm and peaceful, but under the surface is the pain of childbirth, the difficult relationship between Joseph and Mary, the tough journey to Bethlehem, the rejection from the innkeepers when they arrived, the loneliness of being refugees in Egypt, and the guilt of knowing that so many young boys were killed while they survived. Take a moment to tell God about a problem you're facing, and ask him to help you deal with it and to remember you're not alone.

Home prayer

Give or *take* five minutes a day: every person in the family chooses whether they want to give an early Christmas gift or take one.

Give five minutes: give five minutes a day for the week before Christmas to help the busiest person in your family, without waiting to be asked for your help.

Take five minutes: take five minutes every day to stop, remember what is most important in your life, give someone a hug, get some fresh air, deliberately smile, or read a good book.

5

Christmas Extras

Here are some extra ideas to be used whenever you like over the Christmas season. An online search will give you full details that will suit your budget and skills.

- **Wrapping paper and gift tag printing:** Do potato printing or sponge printing; print with shapes cut out of foam or sponges (using a cookie cutter); use metallic paint on a plain background.

- **Card making:** Learn about pop-up card mechanics; use scrapbook embellishments, transfers, punches, and scissors.

- **Christmas tree ornaments:** Make from glittery pipe cleaners, cardstock, wood, felt, or salt dough.

- **Stained-glass decorations:** Color in acetate sheets; or cut shapes out of black cardstock or paperstock and stick tissue paper over them; or cover the gaps with tape and sprinkle colored glitter on to the sticky side. Make "stained-glass cookies" with crushed and boiled candy.

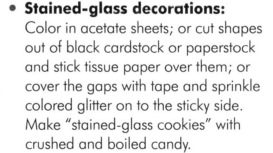

- **Advent candles:** Use permanent markers to mark twenty-four days on a candle (put number one at the top) and light each day.

- **Advent countdown:** Cut a six-inch circle out of a favorite Christmas card. Punch a hole in the top of the circle and thread a festive ribbon through it as a hanger. Make a peg wreath by gluing twenty-four wooden pegs at equal distances around the edge of the circle, each peg holding a cut-out circle with a number from one to twenty-four. Place the number twenty-five in the center of the countdown wreath.

- **Gift containers:** Decorate bags, boxes, envelopes, or packets to hold Christmas gifts.

- **Christmas door wreaths:** Make from natural materials or artificial ones— wind ribbon or strips of cloth around to decorate the background.

- **Paper chains:**
Make chains with stapled links, strips folded over each other, twists, or accordian-style.

- **Candleholders:** Make from old CDs, saucers, glasses, or bottles.

- **Paper party hat or crown:** Design hats in magi style as animal headdresses, angel halos, or turbans.

- **Mobiles:** Design mobiles using stars, nativity characters, or angels.

- **Old Masters paintings:** Print off nativity scenes from Old Masters paintings and replace the visitors to the stable with drawings or photos of yourselves.

- **Carpentry:** Bang nails into wood as if you were in Joseph's shop; learn simple sawing.

- **Sheep:** (1) Make from cotton balls, with googly eyes glued onto a black foam face. (2) Draw around your hand. Color the thumb and fingers black (for the head and four legs), then squirt shaving foam over the palm area, adding black materials for eyes and nose. (3) Make from white marshmallows with small candies for legs and icing for the face.

- **Nativity coloring:** Draw and color your own nativity scenes.

- **Nativity fuzzy felt:** Cut out simple felt shapes to make a stable, nativity figures, and animals. Stick them on sheets of sandpaper.

- **Table centerpiece:** Make a dried flower arrangement.

- **Floating candles:** Make from a non-boiling wax candle kit (the sort you squish in your hand).

- **Table runner:** Make a runner from Christmas-themed cloth.

- **Table placemat:** Color a nativity scene, print it on cardstock, and laminate it.

- **Table place name tags:** Make tags with markers, stamping, stickers, calligraphy, or 3D fabric paint pens.

- **Baby sock angels:** Fill a white baby sock with pillow stuffing and knot or sew up the end. Form a head by tying gold or silver ribbon tight at the neck. Use gold or silver wide wired ribbon tied in a bow to form wings, and make a halo for the head. Decorate the face and add random sticky stars to the body.

- **Centerpiece candles:** Place real or glass pebbles in a glass jar to a depth of two inches. Fill the jar two-thirds up with clean water and place a floating candle on top. Wrap a raffia bow around the jar.

- **Cinnamon candles:** Tie cinnamon sticks around vanilla candles with rustic string or raffia.

- **Shine!** For brighter paintings, mix food coloring with condensed milk and paint with a brush. You'll get fewer drips and a glossy shine.

- **Christmas tree ornaments:** Double up a pipe cleaner and thread buttons onto it to make an angel.

- **Christmas science experiments:** Trace stars or angels on to plastic food containers and bake to shrink; do the Mentos geyser experiment using cola and Mentos; grow crystal star ornaments from chemicals in solution over several weeks; do an online search for "simple Christmas experiments" for more ideas or talk to a science teacher at your local high school. They will have lots of ideas that they are itching to try.

6

Go for a Green Christmas

Here are some ideas for recycling and reusing Christmas cards, paper, and trimmings.

Recycle Christmas cards

- **New cards from old:** Cut out pictures and stick on new scenes to make new cards.

- **Origami boxes:** Fold cards up to make little boxes.

- **Nativity characters:** Cut out card circles and fold them into cone shapes to make nativity characters.

- **Multi-sided decorations:** Cut out circles and stick them together to make Christmas tree ornaments. (Search on the Internet: "recycled Christmas cards ornaments.")

- **Patchwork:** Cut out card hexagons and stick them together to make a patchwork picture.

- **Gift tags:** Cut out shapes with wiggly-edged scissors, or punch them out, to make gift tags. Consider mounting the shapes on to fresh pieces of cardstock.

- **Gift bags:** Cut out shapes and glue them onto plain paper lunch bags to make festive bags.

- **Sewing cards:** Make children's sewing cards by using a small hole punch to outline a shape.

- **Wreath:** Cut out characters from the Christmas story and glue them onto heavy cardstock or foam circles to make a Christmas wreath. Add ribbon to hang up.

- **Flags:** Cut cards into triangles and attach them to colorful ribbon to make flag banners.

- **Paper chains:** Cut into strips to make paper chain links.

- **Bookmarks:** Cut into strips, punch holes, and add lengths of ribbon.

- **Menus:** Cover the inside of the card with green or red paper. Glue a Christmas dinner menu inside and place on the Christmas meal table, or reuse as a Christmas Day invitation.

- **Napkin rings:** Bend strips of cardstock into circles and tape together to make napkin rings.
- **Decoupage:** Set an army of adults to work, cutting out interesting figures, people, patterns, and animals from cards to use as decorative shapes to stick on cards or notebooks.
- **Titles:** Cut cards into letter shapes and use them to add a title to your next wall display.

Reuse old clean wrapping paper

- **Storage:** Cut paper into neat shapes—it's much easier to store and nicer to use.
- **Fan:** Fold a rectangle of paper like an accordian and make it into a fan.
- **Decoupage:** Cut out repeated shapes to decorate cards or notebooks.
- **Gift bags:** Staple sheets together to make bags.
- **Notebooks:** Cover plain notebooks with your favorite wrapping designs.
- **Origami:** Cut into squares or strips and use for origami projects.
- **Bows:** Cut foil wrapping paper into strips and turn them into decorative Christmas bows for gifts or wreaths.
- **Gift pocket:** Cut sturdy paper into two matching star, ornament, or stocking shapes; punch holes around the edges and sew together with a simple whipping stitch, leaving one side open to place a small gift.
- **Packaging:** Shred and use to make bright packaging.
- **Homemade confetti:** Punch out shapes for confetti or mosaics.
- **Shape it:** Cut out shapes using a die-cutting machine.
- **Fun scrap:** Draw around hands or feet and cut out the shapes, just for fun.
- **Housework:** Crumpled wrapping paper is great for cleaning windows. To make a window-cleaning pack, put crumpled paper and a bottle of vinegar in a paper bag decorated with a cut-out of a festive window from an old Christmas card.

Salvage Christmas decorations

Ask people to save all the pretty things that you find on Christmas packaging but that clutter up the house, such as:

- Decorations
- Small toys
- Bows
- Small boxes or bags
- Lengths of ribbon
- Plastic holly or poinsettia sprigs
- Cake decorations (clean)
- Torn or bare tinsel
- Slightly battered ornaments

Sort, box, and label them rigorously and reuse them during the year for interesting messy projects. (Young children don't mind if something has a Christmas look in June.)

Messy Activity Ideas

- **Tracks:** Drive toy cars through paint over large sheets of paper (pretending to be shepherds walking to Bethlehem through mud).

- **Angels:** Make snow angels, waving your arms up and down in shredded paper on the floor instead of snow.

- **Christmas graffiti wall:** Write or draw what's best about Christmas using chalk, paint, or marker pens on a large piece of paper hung on the wall.

- **Wallpaper or paint a wall:** This is great fun in itself, it's a useful life skill, and it ties in with the theme of homes.

- **Upcycle a gift:** Paint a piece of old furniture to make the most of your home.

- **Swing-painting:** Fill a small pot with paint, glitter, sand, or salt, suspend it very close to the floor (a half-inch away), and let it swing over a large sheet of paper. You can create angel dust, the journey of the wise men, or the path of the star.

- **Decorate a person:** Invite people to put as much double-sided tape on two people as they can. Suspend a net full of small scraps of shiny paper, shredded tinsel, or ribbon and, with the "sticky" people gathered below the net, see who gets the shiniest as the pieces shower down on them.

- **Decorate a tree:** Make six-foot cardboard cut-outs of Christmas trees. Using *lots* of glue, decorate them with sackfuls of old Christmas tree decorations that you've collected from the church, old Christmas card pictures, strips of old wrapping paper, ribbon, and tinsel. Tell the story of the first Christmas tree.

- **Glue pictures:** Using a large sheet of plastic as a covering for the floor or table, dot glue over sheets of dark paper and throw handfuls of glitter or white powder paint down on it. Tap off the residue, and the starry sky is before you. Use a similar technique for a wise man's robe with decorative squiggles, or the outline of an angel.

- **Marbled wrapping paper:** Squirt shaving foam onto a wipe-clean surface or table and drip food coloring or paint on top. Mix to make a marbled effect and place sheets of paper on top to print wrapping paper.

- **Hidden stars:** Fix large sheets of paper onto a wall with masking tape. Line the floor below with plastic sheets. Draw stars with white crayons or household candles, then brush over with a black paint wash to "find" the constellations or hidden angels.

- **Big picture:** Mark out an area beneath a balcony or other easily accessible viewpoint. Provide a large pile of colored sheets and a simple picture of the nativity, and invite people to make a huge version of that picture on the ground using the sheets as the blocks of color. View your picture from the balcony.

- **Combo-meditation:** Give each person a circle of a different colored card. Invite them to decorate it with their take on the same Christmas theme, such as "The best thing about Christmas," "New life in God," "The way I feel about Christmas," or "Messy Christmas." Attach the circles to a big backing sheet to make one huge, dramatic piece of artwork.

Global Action and Justice at Christmas

- Charities' websites often suggest really good ideas under "Get involved," "Youth leader resources," "Teachers," or "Fundraising ideas." Try Save the Children, Angel Tree, Heifer International, Toys for Tots, or the Salvation Army.

- Send a neighboring church a Messy Church–made Christmas card.

- Display nativity sets from other cultures, clearly labeled.

- Invite someone from the wider church into Messy Church to do a Christmas activity from their own country.

- If it's too late to send resources overseas, consider going to charities closer to home. Local women's shelters, children's wards in hospitals, or homeless shelters may have specific needs that your Messy Church could help to meet.

- With permission, take a Messy Choir carol-singing in a nursing home and make tiny gifts or cards to give out to the residents there.

- Paint glass ornaments in the shape and color of globes.

Christmas Games

Here are some ideas for games to use up excess energy.

- **Hide and seek from Herod:** Take turns being Herod.

- **"First shepherd to the manger" race:** Make a simple manger from a shoebox.

- **Loudest trumpet blast:** Played by an angel on real trumpet.

- **Longest trumpet blast:** Played by an angel on a party horn.

- **Camel racing:** On piggyback or with cardboard camels.

- **Halo frisbee:** Best played outside.

- **Piñata bashing:** A Mexican Christmas tradition.

- **Design an angel:** Fly the furthest/highest or use Alka-Seltzer rocket technology.

- **Hunt the sheep:** Play tag.

- **Holy family parachute:** Give each person a name—Mary, Joseph, or Jesus—and call out names to run under the parachute. Shout "Bethlehem" and everyone has to run under and catch the edge of the parachute.

- **Three kings parachute:** Give each person the name of a wise man—Caspar, Melchior, or Balthazar. Call out the names to run under the parachute. Shout "Follow the star" and everyone has to run under the parachute.

- **Destroy a hay bale (beware of allergies):** See how high the loose hay will stack.

- **Shooting stars skills:** Throw balls through hoops.

- **Herding sheep:** Divide the group into two teams—sheep and shepherds. All run around until a leader shouts, "Come back." The shepherds hold hands to try to trap the sheep and gather them into a corner. Teams then switch.

- **Tails and stars (giant chutes and ladders):** Paint fifteen by fifteen grids on a large bedsheet. Design donkey tails to slide down and shooting stars to climb up. Play the game in small groups and see who has done the best after each group gets three minutes.

- **Running game:** Play a "running to different areas of the room" game, using different place-names from the Christmas story: Nazareth, Bethlehem, Egypt, and Jerusalem. Add appropriate actions when you call out the names of the different characters:

  - Mary: Rock a baby.
  - Joseph: Saw some wood.
  - "Herod's coming!": Run and hide.
  - "See the baby": Run into the center.
  - Sheep and shepherds: Grab a partner; one goes down on all fours as the sheep, while the other rests their hand on the sheep's head.
  - Wise men: Mime looking at the stars.
  - Star: Run around the room once, making a "neeeeeow" noise.
  - Manger: Lie on your back with arms and legs in the air.
  - Scrub the stable: Scrub the floor.

- **Don't wake Herod!** Everyone sits in a circle with one person (Herod) in the middle and a noisy object (such as a bunch of keys) placed on the ground behind them. The person in the middle covers their eyes. A leader points to someone in the circle, who tries to pick up the noisy object and get back to their place without waking Herod. If Herod hears them and gets up, the object has to be dropped to the ground and the player has to run through their place in the circle and once all the way around, with Herod chasing. They must try to get back to their place before being caught. Swap the Herod every two or three turns, or if someone is caught.

Interactive story: a strange journey

Practice these actions as responses to the words printed in bold in the following story. Then tell the story.

- King/s: Stand and bow.
- Palace: Say, "Oooh" (impressed).
- Camels: Say, "Brr" (a camel noise made by flapping lips).
- Star: Say, "Twinkle, twinkle" (flicking fingers in and out).

- You cannot be serious: Half the congregation says, "Oh yes we can." The others say, "Oh no you can't."
- Count: Shout, "2, 4, 6, 8, who do we appreciate? Jesus!"

Once there was a **king** who lived in a beautiful **palace**. He was named Herod. One day, he'd just been out for a ride on his **camel** when he **counted** three more **kings** on his doorstep. They had been following a bright **star**, which, they said, should lead them to a new **king**. Herod didn't like the idea of new **kings** being born. **"You cannot be serious,"** he said. "But we saw your amazing **palace**," said the wise men, "and thought this must be the place. So, have you got any new babies?"

Herod's advisers pointed to a map and showed the three wise men how to get to Bethlehem. **"You cannot be serious,"** they said. "We've followed this **star** for months and months—too many to **count**." But they jumped on their **camels** and rode away from the magnificent **palace**. They found the **star** floating above a tiny little house in the tiny little town of Bethlehem. The three **kings** were very disappointed indeed, and almost went home again, but instead they rested their **camels** and knocked on the door. A mother opened it with a little child at her feet. They were overjoyed to see Jesus. They gave him presents of gold, frankincense, and myrrh, and knelt down to worship him.

Their strange journey had not been at all what they'd expected, but it had been worthwhile, as it's the birth of our dear Lord that **counts**!

Christmas Food Crafts

- **Sweet presents:** Make candies, cookies, or chocolate treats and wrap them nicely in cellophane.

- **Gingerbread shapes:** Make and decorate.

- **Gingerbread house:** Construct a house out of gingerbread.

- **Christmas crackers:** Decorate cheese crackers with savory red, green, and white foods (green or red peppers, cucumber, raw peas, cream cheese, cottage cheese, mayonnaise, cherry tomatoes, radishes, apples, and so on).

- **Edible crib scene:** Make marshmallow sheep, fondant angels, a pretzel stable, a jelly bean Jesus, and shredded wheat hay.

- **Cookies:** Bake cookies with a Christmas-story theme (star, angel, sheep, crown shapes, etc.).

- **No-bake Christmas cookies:** Search for recipes on the Internet.

- **Miniature Christmas cake:** Decorate a miniature Christmas cake.

- **Glass decoration:** Dip the rim of a damp glass in caster sugar to frost it (egg white is usually suggested, but this carries the risk of salmonella) and make festive cocktails (grape juice and fizzy water).

- **Sparkly cupcakes:** Decorate cupcakes with edible glitter.

- **Icing angels:** Use an icing bag to squirt rosettes of butter icing over an upturned ice cream cone. Add a face made from fondant icing or writing icing.

- **Toast:** Mix yellow food coloring with milk and paint a star on a piece of white sliced bread. Toast in an electric toaster.

- **Toblerone Christmas:** With judicious use of icing you can write with, the triangle shape can be decorated as a Christmas tree, an arrow-shaped sign pointing toward Bethlehem, an angel, or a pyramid (for the story of the flight to Egypt). (Watch out for nut allergies: if necessary, find similar-shaped chocolates without nuts.)

- **No-cook Christmas star cakes:** In a blender, combine mixed dried fruit, ginger, mixed spice, and ground almonds. Add a small amount of orange juice to make small round balls. Form the balls into a flatter shape. Cut star shapes out of marzipan or ready-mixed icing, and place them on top of the cakes. Decorate stars with icing. (Watch out for nut allergies.)

- **Dipped pretzels:** The heart shape and the folded embracing arms in the pretzel remind us how much Jesus loves us. Dip one half in melted white chocolate and the other in melted dark chocolate. The chocolate will dry in five minutes. Gather four or five pretzels and thread ribbon through to make a gift.

Messy Moments Sheets

You might leave these sheets lying around your Messy Church, or encourage families to look at them together, or to take them home to enjoy with members of the family who can't make it to Messy Church.

Advent

Messy gifts

Who do you want God to bless? Color in a gift for them and write their name on the label.

Messy Mary

What is Mary thinking about before she sets off for Bethlehem? Draw or write her thoughts in the bubbles.

Messy family tree

In Matthew's Gospel, we read about Jesus' family tree. Draw some of the people from your family in the second family tree.

Abraham

Rahab

Jesse

David

Joseph — Mary

Christmas

Messy news

The angel said,
"I bring you good news!"

What good news do you want to share?

Fill in this newspaper front page with it.

Messy angels

The angel told the shepherds, "Don't be afraid!" Color in an angel for each thing you're afraid of, and ask God to help you be brave about it.

Messy shed

What do you think it smelled like in the shed where Jesus was born? Color in the smells.

Epiphany

Messy thank you

Color in one letter for everything you're thankful for at the moment.

Messy map

Fill in this messy map with pictures of people on journeys.

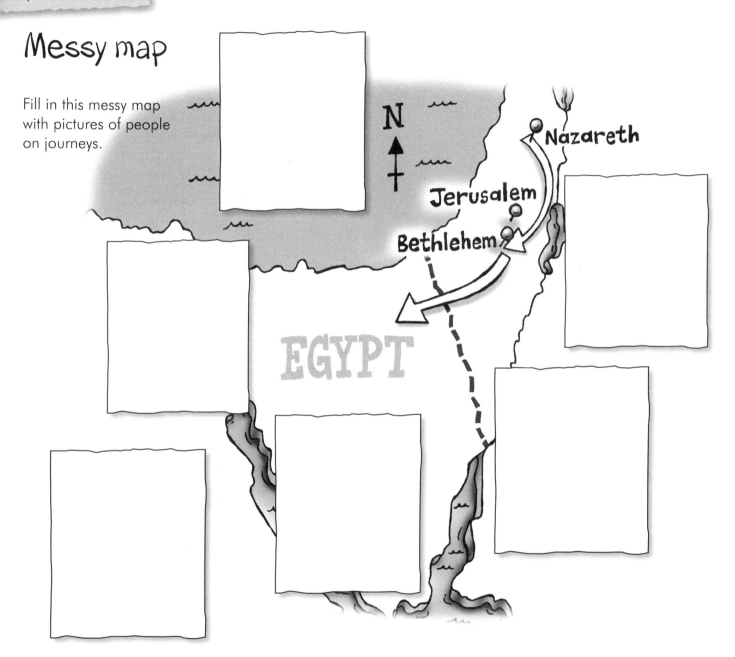

N

Nazareth

Jerusalem

Bethlehem

EGYPT

Messy lights

What lights up this year for you? What are you looking forward to? Draw the different things on the lamp posts.

Index of Crafts and Games

Advent candles............................... 70
Advent countdown........................... 70
Angel costumes.............................. 36
Angels.. 76
Baby sock angels........................... 72
Bath bombs 11
Big picture 77
Bookmarks.................................... 73
Bows 74
Camel racing................................. 79
Candleholders 71
Card making.................................. 70
Carpentry 71
Centerpiece candles 72
Chocolate-covered treats 14
Christmas door wreaths 71
Christmas graffiti wall 76
Christmas science experiments......... 72
Christmas to do list........................ 10
Christmas tree ornaments.......... 70, 72
Cinnamon candles 72
Combo-meditation 77
Cookies.. 82
Decorate a person......................... 76
Decorate a tree 76
Decoupage.................................... 74
Design an angel 79
Destroy a hay bale......................... 79
Dipped pretzels 83
Don't wake Herod 80
Edible crib scene 82

Edible stars 55
Fan 74
Fingerprint family........................... 34
"First shepherd to the manger" race 79
Flags 73
Floating candles 72
Forgiveness plaque......................... 53
Fun scrap..................................... 74
Game: how many people fit
on a donkey?................................ 16
Gift bags 73, 74
Gift containers 71
Gift sachet................................... 74
Gift tags 73
Gingerbread house 82
Gingerbread shapes 82
Glass decoration............................ 82
Glue pictures 77
Halo frisbee 79
Hand massage............................... 49
Herding sheep 79
Hidden stars................................. 77
Hide and seek from Herod 79
Holy family parachute..................... 79
Homemade confetti 74
Homeless collection box.................. 38
Housework 74
Hunt the sheep.............................. 79
Ice sculpture 40
Interactive story 81
Large wreath no. 1 12

Large wreath no. 2 33
Large wreath no. 3 52
Longest trumpet blast.............................. 79
Loudest trumpet blast.............................. 79
Marbled wrapping paper 77
Menus... 73
Miniature Christmas cake.......................... 82
Mirror mobile.. 51
Mobiles 71
Multi-sided decorations............................. 73
Napkin rings 74
Nativity characters 73
Nativity coloring-in 71
Nativity fuzzy felt...................................... 71
New cards from old 73
No-bake Christmas cookies 82
No-cook Christmas star cakes 83
Notebooks.. 74
Old Masters paintings............................... 71
Origami 74
Origami boxes 73
Packaging.. 74
Paper chains 71, 73
Paper party hat/crown.............................. 71
Patchwork 73
Pillowcases/stockings 13
Piñata bashing 79
Rough log slab stools............................... 19
Running game... 80
Salty house 49
Sewing cards.. 73
Shape it... 74

Sheep.. 71
Shelter for the homeless 32
Shepherds picture.................................... 35
Shine!.. 72
Shooting stars skills.................................. 79
Sparkly cupcakes...................................... 82
Stained-glass decorations.......................... 70
Stir-fry vegetable chopping 15
Straw bed 31
Sweet presents 82
Swing-painting 76
Table centerpiece 71
Table placemat... 72
Table place name tags............................... 72
Table runner... 72
Tails and stars 79
Tea light holders....................................... 48
Thank you notes.. 47
Three kings parachute................................ 79
Titles 74
Toast 82
Toblerone Christmas 83
Tracks.. 76
Upcycle a gift... 76
Upcycle wooden items 18
Wall display/bulletin board.............. 17, 37, 54
Wallpaper/paint a wall 76
White Christmas from Australia.................... 39
Wise man's star bookmark 50
Wrapping paper and gift tag printing 70
Wreath 73

ALSO AVAILABLE

Messy Church
978-0-8308-4138-7

Messy Easter
978-0-8308-4140-0

Doing church differently

BRF's Messy Church is a form of church that involves creativity, celebration, and hospitality, and enables people of all ages to belong to Christ together through their local church. It is particularly aimed at people who have never belonged to a church before.

Find out more at **messychurch.org.uk**.

 brf.org.uk